My National Parks

Susan Thames

Rourke
Publishing LLC
Vero Beach, Florida 32964

www.rourkepublishing.com

PHOTO CREDITS: Cover: © Stephen Hoerold; page 9: © Jose Antonio Santiso Fernandez; page 10: © David Rose; page 11: © Kate Leigh; page 12: © Anton Foltin; page 13: © Leng Chang; page 14: © Mike Morley; page 15: © Eric Foltz; page 20: © Christine Balderas

Editor: Robert Stengard-Olliges

Cover design by Nicola Stratford

Library of Congress Cataloging-in-Publication Data

Thames, Susan.
  My national parks / Susan Thames.
     p. cm. -- (The world around me)
  ISBN 1-59515-995-9 (Hardcover)
  ISBN 1-59515-966-5 (Paperback)
  1. National parks and reserves--United States--Juvenile literature. I. Title.
  E160.T47 2007
  917.3'04931--dc22

                              2006022157

Printed in the USA

CG/CG

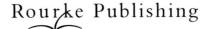

Rourke Publishing

www.rourkepublishing.com – sales@rourkepublishing.com
Post Office Box 3328, Vero Beach, FL 32964

Table of Contents

Our National Parks

National Parks can be found from the rocky coast of Maine to the roaring volcanoes of Hawai'i. The National parks are open to the public and owned by all the people. They are places where the land and all animals are protected.

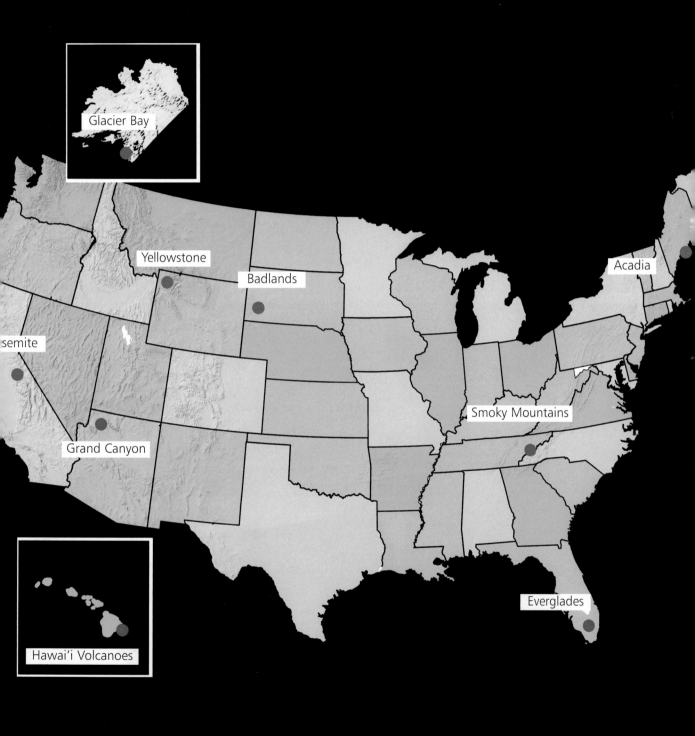

Glacier Bay

Yellowstone

Badlands

semite

Grand Canyon

Acadia

Smoky Mountains

Hawai'i Volcanoes

Everglades

Acadia National Park

Acadia National Park is located along the coast of Maine. Acadia has rocky coasts, waves, forests, and tidepools. You can fish, swim, and boat in the cold water around the park.

Acadia

Everglades National Park

Everglades National Park is located in Florida. It has **marshes** and forests of cypress and pine trees. Crocodiles, alligators, and manatees make their home in the Everglades. Many visitors canoe and hike through the park's trails.

Everglades →

Great Smoky Mountains National Park

Great Smoky Mountains National Park is located on the border between Tennessee and North Carolina. Bears, foxes, and deer make their home in the forest. There are many hiking trails throughout the park.

Smoky Mountains

Grand Canyon National Park

The Grand Canyon is located in northwest Arizona. It is a spectacular canyon with colorful rock walls that are more than a mile high. People can explore the canyon with a mule ride.

Grand Canyon

Badlands National Park

The Badlands are located in South Dakota. The unique land formations are full of fossils and were created by **erosion**. In the summer you can see **paleontologists** digging for fossils at the "Big Pig Dig."

Badlands

Yellowstone National Park

Yellowstone National Park was the first national park. The park has glaciers, **geysers** and hot springs. Bison, grizzlies, and elk roam the green forests and snowcapped mountains.

Yellowstone

Glacier Bay National Park

Glacier Bay National Park is located in Alaska. The park has a rugged landscape of coastal beaches, **fjords**, glaciers, forests and snowcaped mountains. Most visitors to Glacier Bay tour the park from large cruise ships.

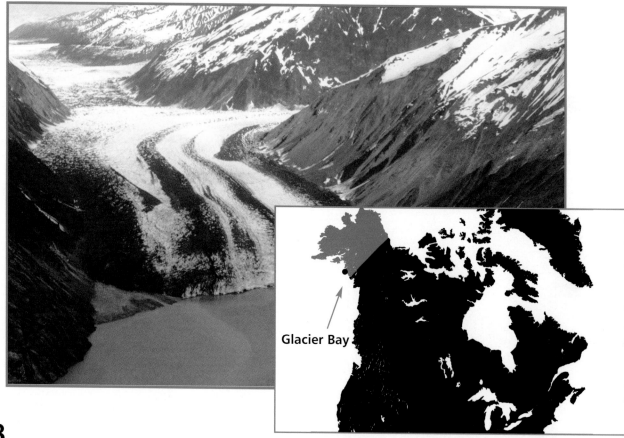

Glacier Bay

Yosemite National Park

Yosemite National Park is located in California. It has giant Sequoia trees, thundering waterfalls and rock cliffs. In early summer you can see fields of wildflowers.

Yosemite

Hawai'i Volcanoes National Park

Hawai'i Volcanoes National Park is located on the Big Island of Hawai'i. The park includes Kilauea the Earth's most active volcano. Visitors view hot **lava** as it flows from Kilauea and other volcanoes into the Pacific Ocean.

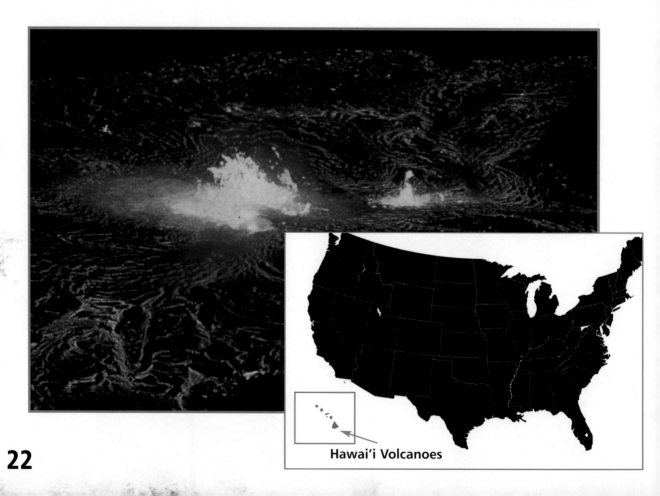

Hawai'i Volcanoes

GLOSSARY

erosion (I ROH zhuhn) - the movement of rocks and soil on the earths surface by wind, water, and ice.

fjords (FYORD) - long, narrow deep inlet with steep sides

geyser (GYE zur) - spring that shoots out hot water and steam.

lava (LAH va) - melted rock that flows from a volcano

marsh (MARSH) - soft, wet grassy land

paleontologist (pale ee uhn TOL uh jist) - someone who studies acient life

INDEX

FURTHER READING

Domeniconi, David. *M is for Majestic: a National Parks Alphabet*. Sleeping Bear Press. 2003.

Graf, Mike. *Everglades National Park*. Bridgestone Books, 2004.

Hall, Margaret. *Glacier National Park*. Heinemann Library, 2006.

WEBSITES TO VISIT

www.nps.gov

www.takepride.gov

www.wikipedia.org/wiki/hawaii-volcanoes-national-park

ABOUT THE AUTHOR

Susan Thames, a former elementary school teacher, lives in Tampa, Florida. She enjoys spending time with her three grandsons and wants to instill in them a love of reading and a passion for travel.